M. J. Scott

Copyright 2018

Daniel Wetta Publishing

Other Books by M. J. Scott, USA

Double Feature!

Sport's Alien Fantasy (Co-author Daniel Wetta)

Power Steering 2

Power Steering

Time on the Turn

Journey into Fulfillment

Visit Author Website:
www.danielwetta.com/powersteeringus

Visit Author Amazon Central Page: www.amazon.com/M.-J.-Scott/e/B06XGJMMKN

DEDICATION

This little book, *Finding the Spirit of Christmas,* is
for the author an invisible gathering of blessings
and bouquets of various shades of life which I
am gifting to all who are anxious and tired in
their spirits and who need the refreshment of
grace.

*Especially for Erma
and family.
Sharing life and
friendships is a key
Blessing.
Marilyn*

TABLE OF CONTENTS   Page

FINDING THE SPIRIT OF CHRISTMAS

DECEMBER 1.

Catching the Christmas Spirit is a grasp of feeling beyond explanation, but when it captures us, we experience life in a newness of joy that displays itself in the steps of our paces and the lights on our faces!

This year it took me in a siege on Thanksgiving Day in the after-joy of witnessing our family actor on Merchant's Square in Williamsburg. He is our Christmas Carol of Charles Dickens' famed old spirit, which is still alive today, and our protagonist took center stage. Only this time of year does he act - and he is no less than Scrooge!

Ah, Merchant's Square! The reflections of the showcases with clear images of Christmas urgings and strong, vibrant reflections of branching trees and colonial chimneys! The camera caught those to enjoy later, and, today while reviewing, I saw one showcase that displayed a beautiful sweater beckoning to be purchased. So, back to Merchant's Square, and it got packaged in a charmingly masculine-gift-wrapped box which found a snug tuck under this author's arm and then was placed on the top shelf to wait the perfect time for giving. But, no, there was a strange urge to take it down and return it for someone else's joy, replacing it with a first-time-ever - a Christmas gift in certificate form. It was so light as it drifted into my hand. I went off to find the perfect Christmas card to accompany it.

Yes, the favorite Barnes & Noble bookstore had roadway priority, and, yes, the prayed-for parking spot was ready, too. I breathed my gratitude, "Thank you, Lord."

Walking through the store, I took in the shelves and innumerable rows of gift ideas, but there was only one place to find the perfect card. Awaiting me as I approached, it spoke softly, "Pick me." It highlighted a dancing deer in snowflake happiness.

Then the stop for picking up a newly framed picture for a birthday-later surprise. The day was wheeling by, and I returned home again for a short time-out.

Check the Incoming box of e-mail - nothing waiting. Check the Sent box of yesterday, and these seemed to still be in queue. What? Suddenly, the cause revealed itself: The airplane mode had accidentally been hit on the cell phone, and everything was in waiting mode. Hmm, Christmas Spirit is flying, but I need some ground support, please!

Later, I felt the nudge to check the incoming box again, and there was the most desired signature checking in. So, giggles of mischief led to a reply of happenings. From me escaped a sigh wishing that the Spirit of Christmas just might ring in a lovely sounding voice later.

Earlier today, the Spirit of Christmas was also in play when, in picking up a framed gift, I asked a lady getting into her car next to mine, "Have you ever seen how their framing looks?"

"No!"

"Oh, may I show you?" She looked with surprise and delight upon my canvas picture and frame. I thanked her for indulging me in sharing.

The computer screen that showed the yesterday-missing messages soon brought a cherished voice. Laughing, joking and sharing - that's the Christmas Spirit unleashed. So, the next adventure will be to leave the shop window reflections and search the consignment stores and shopping malls for the Christmas Spirit shining.

I mustn't forget to report that the Pastor sent an email message with a huge rainbow adorning the sky just above our church. That, too, was a Christmas promise in rainbow color hues. Do we develop a sensitivity for joy in even just the little things?

And yet another invitation to meet family members while on holiday visiting.

Now we have sharing and visiting to add to the output of the Christmas Spirit. This shopping cart will be light except when reams of printing paper require a renewed stack. So, for tonight, we have started our trek into the holidays searching for luminescent images that display the Christmas Spirit. Oh, yes, and tomorrow battery candles must be located. To be continued…

Hello again, it's me!

By now you must know that you are invited to explore with me in the search for the Spirit of Christmas. Be careful, it can be fragile. It just dodged me and jumped several lines ahead in my writing before stopping. Sometimes, it is a little hard to hold onto. But, let's try! We aren't going to compete with "The Twelve Days of Christmas," because this is the first day of December. My 12 days are all in little boxes waiting to be opened patiently.

To begin, let's allow our thoughts to wander in memory and emerge with wonderful stories to share. Phone calls count in the sharing of the Christmas Spirit. My ears are still ringing from a surprise "real live" phone call last night. So, let's add phone calls to our list of good ways to share. You just might want to keep your own list as we pull up our stockings. That's a great idea, and while you are thinking what to stuff, get those ready to hang somewhere. I guarantee these will be filled with joy. Will they be homemade things that come out of your treasure chest? Another good idea is to get out your pen and paper and start a list of precious family and friends who will receive notes from you. Don't forget to stop by the post office and buy more postage stamps - your choice on the design of the stamps.

Okay, laugh and say that's an old-fashioned thing and that emails are easier. Better plan time to do both! The written notes have almost disappeared from our society of high tech. Let's try the new and keep tradition alive, too.

This is a tough assignment, because in the excitement of writing about this, extra letters seem to keep shooting from my fingertips. All this is a juggle, but in the end, it's like standing in front of the candy store and feeling sugary. Good mischief delivered with giggles will help keep the Spirit alive during our December of living. To maintain the Spirit is very important.

Hearts really can burst with an unfolding of profound happiness!

Time out for breakfast coffee which still must be made. Do you like French toast? Using cinnamon bread is a touch of holiday trickery. The recipe will slow us down in our writing, for extra letters fly out when eggs, milk and vanilla jump into the bowl during a writing session! Elves can be sneaky!

I hope you are having fun in our escapade of tossing ingredients in the kitchen. Sometimes there is a stroke of luck to find a whim in the pantry to throw in! That brings up making cookies. Think about whom you might invite to a cookie party. Adding Russian Teacakes is an easy addition. Gentlemen and ladies, you all can get into this merry-making of baking and small time-outs.

Good gracious, thinking is required in this trek through the holidays, so put on your best hat or scarf and keep the head warm. That's right, warmth and happiness accompany us on the right road.

Document recovery just jumped out of hiding, so this may mean our venturing will be like the hide and seek we used to play in the moonlight. Did you hide behind a tree? That reminds me, we can't forget to look for a lovely pine tree just the right size. My dream tree is one growing with its own little roots after being carefully carried home. There's the perfect place for it beside the patio winter garden that is still waiting for pieces of gravel, garden soil and the herbs that were all sold out. Have you seen the cute little rosemary trees? Those would make a great kitchen touch on the counter beside those other delicacies.

Now let's open the shutters onto this new day. The sky is fashioned in horizontal shades of grey, orange, pink and blue. This sky imposes no limits on our day to come of taking small risks by smiling at strangers. Yesterday, a gentleman walking up said, "Did you find everything alright?" I had just come from the tax collector's office. I laughed and told him, "I didn't owe anything on my business license." So, a brief conversation ensued, and I learned that he is a poet and writes for a little across-the-river newspaper and that he knows a friend of mine. I'm not usually that open to strangers, but the intuitive kicked in and reminded me of the spirit of the season. He drove away in his truck of encouraging poetry.

In a small town, there's almost a 99.9% chance that someone knows someone in common. That's why I live in this little tourist mecca, Williamsburg, in the state of "Virginia is for Lovers." That little memory jag brought up the slogan which fits our season of Christmas. (Sorry, I used the slang "jag." I didn't want it to get caught in juggling words.)

Pardon my directness, but I'm so enjoying just talking with you, my reader. Good old-fashioned conversation is very special, so, just for a little, while can you join in?

Goodness, 1,519 words in this new tome, and we have only just begun! We certainly are building a stack of things to watch for this month! Music, please!

Mmm, catch the aroma of a freshly opened container of French roast coffee. Aromas are non-calorie sensations. Breathe deeply! Aromas are blends of life's smells, memories and hopes for a future that feeds the soul. Outside, the sky is filling up with golden hues as the sun melts the fingers of frost from the windshields.

Would you believe it? After I shut the computer down, I found "Christmas Spirit" printed on a big heavy grocery bag. Musicians, costumed ladies and gentlemen ready for a concert, snowflakes and messages that spring into dancing on a bag of delights. We aren't the only ones who are still looking for more sharing of the Christmas Spirit.

Okay, out the door. Ignition and key meet with great gusto, and we are off and down the street past a very large bank decorated with huge wreaths and red bows in every window. The entrance way is wearing swags of pine and ribbons. Such a visual delight!

I have always loved driving just for the romance of viewing the surroundings. Some of my road trips have been long. Remember when the backseat passengers used to say, "Are we there yet?" "Nope!" would be the response, or maybe something more in line with family annoyance. I just heard a memory giggle - did you have this experience too?

Stopping at my home bank to drop off envelopes, I get a good taste of holly-piercing from prickly branches overhanging the parking space. "Ouch!" But then I see happy faces and meet a special young lady with a big hug just for me. These are the things that make our hometown so special. We exchanged compliments and laughed that it would be fun to go shopping together. She looked like she had just stepped out of a New York modeling agency and was ready for a show window as a live mannequin.

On to the next moment of merriment, which was to admire a huge poinsettia sitting elegantly on a counter next to my "encounter" with friends in the store. In sharing moments with them, I almost forgot the shampoo to accompany the conditioner. It didn't matter.

11

Definitely, sharing is on the Christmas Spirit list, and everything else falls into place.

After that, on to a lovely consignment store in search of the perfect antique picture frame. None appeal in this whole showroom of Christmas on display as I march to the holiday music.

So, we try another antique store, and the picture frames are either too large, too expensive, or just not right for my mood. The lovely lady at the counter tries several versions of suggestions while my mind traces her lovely face, lengthy greying hair, long dress and melting smile. I tell her my mission. She responds, "It's always Christmas in here!"

Wow! She spoke magic words. In a turn-around instant, the curious old-fashioned candle lantern nearby catches my imagination. I purchase it along with four little 4x6 inch glass windows with snowflakes. I place pictures in between these and tape them. With three tiny unlit candles and a little toss of colored floss, these are ready for a surprise visit. Tomorrow we will be off to the colonial cobblestone street for a delivery of these to the Millinery Shop. They are a unique gift for a special lady dressed in 18th century finery with embroidery needle in hand. She's from a very large city and loves to come to our town and share her knowledge. Christmas Spirit is her framed smile as a gift to all of us.

Let's slow down a bit. December first is about to close for the day, and we have a lot more sightseeing this month. Christmas Spirit, you are a companion that can't be bought but can be shared to the millions for free.

"Thank you, Father, for this miracle of today." You may wonder about my word choice of "Father." That's our heavenly Father who listens and watches all, even when Elantra had all green stoplights today except for one. A Christmas mini-miracle in clogging traffic!

You see, I have this frequent sharing of conversation with "Our Father," because I've lacked a father model in my life since age eleven when my father departed this earthly presence. Oh, revelation has now entered our Christmas Spirit list. Amazing!

Three hours later, and I'm wondering where gratitude fits into this painting of Christmas spirit. I needed a jug of spring water and ran to a nearby grocery, one that is rarely on my radar screen. As I was leaving, I saw a young man with whom I had chatted at a checkout register last summer. He had given me a store coupon, and I had said, "I'll check on you!" He was also a full-time student. Well, this evening my surprise came in the parking lot when I saw this young man at this different store. I called out, "Hey, I haven't seen you in a long time!" He smiled a big grin as he pushed a long line of grocery carts with his one-and-half limbs. Was his smile one of gratitude for a simple recognition?

This has been a full day of wonder, surprises and joy. Now it's time to just release these little miracles into a pillowcase to fill like Santa's bag for later. I have a last conscious thought: The boxwood wreaths did smell divine today.

Our first day is recorded in almost 2,400 words. How's your speedy reading? My speed-reading lessons were learned a long time ago when pilots took the course, but I knew it was perfect for better skills in women too!

It was a breathless day. Tomorrow we have another day of charged explorations. Rest well!

DECEMBER 2.

Meditation:

The gentle quiet of night speaks of the "Silent Night," when angels were singing. When will these beautiful lyrics be heard? What day and night? Let's wait and see. In wondering about the miracles of Christmas and the coming birth, the question forms: When the manger hay was arranged for that wee one, did it have the fragrance of sweet clover?

What were the thoughts as the little mother-to-be plodded through the long December days? Did she wonder if they would ever get to Bethlehem as she felt the weight inside her of the man-God bundle of love?

Surely, that donkey ride didn't hold any luxury for the chosen one who was preparing for His own guiding journey. The donkey and reins had been ready, but the skyway had not yet shown them the marking path. We'll just have to remain vigilant for a desert star to rise.

It is December 2, and we are again searching for the Christmas Spirit.

16

"Good Morning, Father, we have a white old-fashioned square lantern and two shining glass snowflake sleeves protecting photographs for someone special, the elegant lady in the millinery shop in Colonial Williamsburg. I offer this prayer in the hope the lady of refinement will accept her pictures placed inside this rustic, unlit gift. I had so much fun shopping and designing it."

Fun! That's it…fun! Today we will seek it.

Story of Bethlehem thoughts returning…

Could Joseph have had thoughts, too, this new-to-be father of earthly responsibility questioning his role? This strapping tall man of carpenter strength and rough hands. How was he going to manage the birthing? He had bathed a little lamb once, and it had wriggled with little blats of glee.

Would heaven's child cry or quietly close His eyes feeling the warm water of His baptism? Joseph patted the mother's shoulder in reassurance that all would be well. He was praying that angels would assist to find blankets

17

for nightly protection from chill. He yearned for splendor of song.

Have we ventured too far into this mystery? Let's return to the twenty-first century.

The unplanned and unexpected just joined forces with the camera lens. Giant rays of sunlight course through the window pane and stretch over a crystal flower vase that converts streaks of yellow into mystical shapes of color. Two rainbows arch on the wall, and, in closer view, they make a shape of angel wings and a torso! This is not imagination, as this has been captured by the digital tell-tale of my camera in the now! We'll just play with the thoughts that Christmas Spirit is very much alive and may pop up again and again!

Hello, are we still on the same channel?

My word, the computer really keeps track of my starts and stops. It just informed me that it has been six hours and twenty-seven minutes since I last spent time on *The Spirit of Christmas.*

The interim was well spent in the afternoon finding one parking spot not sunk in a big black puddle hole. I walked along the brick lane and crossed Duke of Gloucester Street. The familiar name for locals is DOG Street. People love to stroll this colonial capital with their well-groomed best friends. And today, truly, my all-time-favorite dogs were present, sitting ever so quietly with mouths salivating for more treats from passersby. A big chocolate dog and one like a huge lump of coal were sitting with tongues ready to slurp my extended hand. Here were the most loving dogs in my world - the big "Newfies" (Newfoundlands) with huge paws, laughing eyes and, oh my, a great big Christmas package of love in the photograph I snapped. So many treats awaited the stroll down the colonial road with stops to see family members and visits with friends. Please agree that this was a special afternoon.

I did encounter a Scrooge when, upon arriving home, I found that my usual parking spot was coveted by others. The message was, "They want you to use another space." The conversation was courteous and graceful on the surface, but I realized that my shopping cart and

I would have to find another convenient space. I just hope that my old broken shoulder and contrary hip will not find the new trek to my door a misery in negotiating.

I am reminded of the old hymn, "Onward Christian Soldiers," but back in the comfort of my home, I'd rather be listening to "White Christmas" in high definition sound, or, better yet, "Silent Night," to put us back on our Christmas journey. Mary and Joseph didn't have earphones to listen to music on their tiring trek across sand and rocky spots. Did they hear a cry of a far-off coyote or the wind making whistling sounds? Our meditation leads us to try to feel what they experienced and wondered about the unknown just ahead of them. When "No room at the inn" was discovered, the tired travelers realized that even the haven of a stable filled with animal sounds and scents would be a respite from the chill of night.

The pains of birthing became a blessed relief to the weary mother and uneasy father. It signaled the end of their journey and uncertainty. Imagine the deep wells of joy when they heard the first small cry, maybe a little laugh, emitting from the new bundle from heaven! The babe was signaled as a heaven-sent blessing as angels filled the lofty spaces in watchful protection. Far above in the heavens' heights, a star had risen above their stable dwelling. Truly, the star of Bethlehem lit a guiding path for the curious shepherds. The three Wise Men from afar began their journey, too, with a message to keep on and not report to the king. In our story language, we'll just describe that king as a scrooge of bad intent.

If you think this author is being awfully bold, well, it's a gesture of sharing a life-changing event for us all to contemplate. Go check out the exact words in the descriptions of the birth of Jesus for all nations. My expression of this miracle is for the purpose of highlighting the origin of the spirit of Christmas.

Okay, time for donning the garb of sleepy time. We will return to our search tomorrow. First, however, I'll read over this manuscript of our original Christmas gift from keyboard view.

"Thank you, Father, for your watchful eye on this fragile attempt to give Christmas Spirit a boost of energy. Weaving the far-distant years into the enterprising now is a step-by-step effort, like that of the donkey with a burden in my story. But, for tonight, I am spent, and the birth of living thought can now reach out for someone else to carry a while."

Good night!

But wait! For me tonight, I have one last experience, and a little flood of tears have formed across the phone wires with a dear neighbor who has called me. She has just lost her precious love, and yet she took time to call and thank me for the purple orchid I had sent. That's a Spirit of Christmas amid grief-stricken loss.

DECEMBER 3

Have you ever watched the morning breaking into day with a gentle lift from earth into skyward time? Then stand up and watch the colors grow into the crimson loveliness of day's first thirsty breath of beauty? Maybe this ground-breaking is like catching the Spirit of Christmas from the very heart of living.

Spirit is a lighter-than air-burden when accepted with outstretched willingness to accept this dawning of brilliance.

Light, but strong. It lifts heavy loads just as the little donkey trudging to Bethlehem. We're winding our way back into the manger scene. In the chill, the animals' breaths create little clouds around their bodies. Illuminations of daybreaks warm the tangible waiting until the Wise Men appear, adding their gifts of love and respect for the new Messiah.

This gigantic word, "Love," can permeate the world if all hands would be extended from a touch originating from the Gift in the manger. The first capture of the feeling of the Spirit of

Christmas came from the clover essence of heaven's touch.

Let's try today to feel in sensing touch the beauty of smiles and hugs and become wiser in our encounters. The light of day is growing brighter, and time is providing space to add dimensions of greater happiness. Welcome to picking up where we left off!

The star of Bethlehem was a guiding signal for the Wise Men, and, believe it or not, my guiding sky picture appeared today. There, in a blue heaven, appeared a perfectly designed cloud of a flying marlin. The giant swordfish had a large spiny and feathery tail, a shapely body for any fisherman's delight and the long sword nose to slice through the heavenly seas. I felt it a sign that travels through refreshing, cool days lie ahead of me.

Today, the three lanes of highway led to the furniture store that I wanted to check out. Yes, I needed a sofa, so I had taken a pretty colorful napkin of colors holding sway to butterflies and flowers. The thought was maybe to find a maroon shade to compliment the living room.

In walking up to the rotating doors, there waiting was the word, "Gratitude." My goodness, this was a signal to enter and take in my surroundings slowly.

A pretty young sales lady approached me with the normal introduction, "May I help you?"

"Oh, do you have a maroon sofa on sale?"

She replied with a smile, "Come along with me. We have just one!"

There it was! Next Saturday, it will be delivered. In the midst of the transaction, I asked if she were a writer.

"No, I'm a water-color artist."

I asked her to show me some of her work, and these promptly appeared on her cellphone screen. So, an author and a water-color artist struck up a mutual artistic exchange. I felt that her Chinese watercolors and calligraphy would pique my deeper artistic yen. I'm certain we will meet again. Her sunflowers and iris waving from the canvas look three-dimensional. Maybe she will give our books a little star-like thought.

Yes, I felt gratitude, and to me the store was filled with Christmas in motion.

Later today, I wrote a long account of how the intuitive was this afternoon denied. This article will appear in *Power Steering 3*, because we can't derail from our tracks of finding the Christmas Spirit. But I have proof that negative forces aren't happy with chasing Christmas Spirit and placing it tenderly on this page in time. I had no time for negativity, so I took time out to take a deep breath of the wintery season becoming illuminated!

I had just moved on to answering an email, and, suddenly, there appeared this magnificent set of "God's Workshop" pictures. The title was, "Does God Ever Run Out of Ideas?" The photos of exotic gardens graced my screen. They had been forwarded to over twenty-five friends who are always on the go, like me. If they, in turn, would forward these gardens of tropical splendor, then what exponential enhancement of Christmas Spirit contagion could take place!

As I busy myself in my home, I listen to music or let television programs accompany me with human voices. There's so much energy to be absorbed from the transmissions of music and messages through the airwaves and wireless bursts. As I listened today, JOY was felt when a young pastor began to interview his beloved wife about her life and behind-the-scenes-pastoral work. His recognition of her importance brought me a sense of satisfaction and feeling of pride to be one of their unseen friends. I had a vision that they would hold hands leaving the stage, and this they did. I feel like they have touched my heart personally. Joy can spring big from little moments. If we take the moment to notice, we experience the renewal of energy and hope that joy brings. In effect, we experience Christmas Spirit.

Today is closing, but it has shown the strong and light power of spirit.

I hope you will join in tomorrow's continuance of the search for Christmas Spirit and the enjoyment of unexpected gifts!

DECEMBER 4

"Pick up where you left off yesterday," a voice told me upon awakening.

The magic of unparalleled truth and wisdom displays in our arising morning sky. It reminds us of the morning after the great and conscious birth of our Lord. You may give Him the name of your best choice, but, for me, He is Savior from slavery's clutches.

"The Light of the World shone round about." The master builders of land did not see the event of His birth. It was just another day of brick making to them. So, let's move on into our day of now and discover what are the varied tasks set before us.

For this author, it's a climb out of the chair and footstool of elevated comfort to move on into the day with the lightning of enthusiasm. Enthusiasm lightens our loads, whatever these may be. Goodness, the punctuation leaves a reminder of spelling and question marks, too. I try to express things well. What I want you to know is that enthusiasm is in abundance;

hidden, but easily accessed; and it will work for our benefit if we take but a moment to remember to put it on.

However, sometimes we misplace our purpose and are left unprepared. Ouch, that's like the cutting edges of the vase that conked my head yesterday. No, I'm not a sore sport - just experiencing a little ego-smashing dint. But let's shake off temporary blows and recover our enthusiasm!

Now the sun's brightening light is climbing above the clouds and giving sway to Sunday. Time now to break the fast of yesterday and find new clues about the Spirit of Christmas. When I turn on the computer to start the day, I know the message screen will say, "Welcome!"

This morning in the announcements at church, it was briefly mentioned that it was the pastor's birthday. He stood and said, "Yes, birthdays are precious to me, because ten years ago I almost didn't make it to the next birthday!" The organist began to play, "Happy Birthday," but the congregation, still surprised by his statement, sat silently, watching the pastor's reaction. Excuse me, but I just had to stand up in the back row and signal to my friend seated next to me to stand also. Across the sanctuary, someone else noticed, and, suddenly, the whole congregation stood in profound respect and delight and sang. That wave of energy and love added a dimension of Spirit and togetherness. This isn't a boast or brag session. This is honesty that sometimes we have to stand on our own two feet regardless of what others do. So, this author found the birthday experience just as warming as writing about the vigil that the Wise Men kept. They were observing a birthday, too!

In another decision about preparing for the holidays, rather than taking a lunch break, I decided that the Elantra would take me to a well-advertised store with lots of sales to deck the holidays. As the electronic door opened rapidly, I could feel my facial expression as the question formed: Is this a good idea? But, on with the shopping cart to carry a few well-chosen items and then back towards the checkout counter. Wow! Where does that begin and end? The line curved and twisted around several aisles with only two checkout counters open. Imagination caught a thought that there must be over a thousand dollars waiting to be carded. So, I pushed my cart into a little space among the ornament finery, and left it to await another lucky shopper. My selections would be for them, all carefully chosen and ready for their magic touch.

My car was patiently waiting, and we took a gentle exit onto the curving road to home. I checked the emails, and a new little set of adventures came to light. Spirit of Christmas is an awesome high that creates a sense of living to the fullest.

As the reader, have you suddenly found awareness of deep wells of caring? This morning, they were collecting contributions for the Motel Ministry, which is a subtle name for outreach to the homeless. Volunteering to serve these deserving, but unfortunate, individuals supports their next steps to independence. Stop and look around. Do you see any faces of weariness and bags full of earthly weight? Spirit, we have added caring to our stocking of holding Christmas in high regard.

What tomorrow may bring before our eyes could be amazing.

Wait, something special was forgotten! Here on my digital camera is a precious picture taken this morning. A beautiful young mother and her baby daughter were in the entry hall of the church. I asked if I could take their picture? The young mother with a favorite name smiled and sat down in the waiting rocking chair. Moments of waiting for the camera to get out of sleeping mode, and then, just as the picture was tapped into focus, the baby turned with a big quizzical smile. Oh, so perfect, this smiling arrival of a baby in the Spirit of Christmas. Yes, unforgettable!

There was talk of a cold-front storm to arrive tonight. As the clouds thickened in readiness, I had noticed the birds flocking closer together. From my window, I saw a lone leader get the flock into formation. It was like a practice, because then they glided to their branches for the evening approaching. The role of leadership can be daunting in thought but a natural component of being observant.

Returning to the present, I hear an unexpected sound beating against the windows. I go in search. The approaching rainstorm is here so early? I turn on the stairway light and head downstairs, open the patio door and find that the sound is much farther out of reach. Stepping outdoors, I have a skyward view provided by winter, because the trees in the adjacent park have released their leaves. There was the sound I had been hearing, and the sound itself seemed to light up the sky in bursts of pink, green and golden star explosions. Ah! Colonial Williamsburg's "Grand Illumination," the Christmas display of fireworks that grace the wintry nights every December! Tens of thousands come to see the lights of colonial times in the candlelit windows of houses adorned with handcrafted fruit wreaths. The fireworks are to make a special night for families and friends braving the chill and clustering around the warming fires in order to see the celestial show. For me on my distant patio, it was a little feast of a concert in the sky. The rains had waited until the seasonal exhibit of lights and celebration would be enjoyed. Yes, enjoyment is the legacy of a gift to the community from a host that honors history every year at the opening of the holidays in our colonial town. Center among the crowds are love, hope and life! On my patio, I whisper, "Thank you for such a Sunday, just one of a kind every year."

Throughout Williamsburg and the world this early December night, the heart and passion of Christmas are being shared in great concerts and musicals. There are rhythms that touch heart, body and soul and illuminations to brighten our lives.

Once, in a lively discussion group, I heard, "Music is a universal language, and perhaps this will melt our nations into recognizing one voice." As the holy days of Advent move closer to the star's appearance announcing Christ's birth, let's pass through simple doors that open into concerts resounding of Peace.

I close my evening with a recollection of one recent early morning awakening to words of gifts. My family had come together for Thanksgiving, and they were already stirring to begin the preparations for the Thanksgiving table. Coffee, busyness and then, inevitably, the conversation turned to Christmas and what would be the exchange of gifts. That topic had popped in and out throughout the morning unresolved, but at the Thanksgiving table, my son-in-law said, " Let's just give each other one gift this year for Christmas. Let's just have food, fun, fellowship and friendship as family gifts." The penetrating silence that followed gave way to sighs of delight around our table of blessings. We all suddenly saw that the gift of sharing would be the most meaningful gift of our season. Surprise and gratitude arrived at our table ahead of the Thanksgiving plates of festive food.

Let's remember to create those precious moments in time when the togetherness of family can be exposed to laughter, joy and conversations that open doors. So, instead of hours of shopping and wrapping of presents, we will have greetings of open arms, hugs of thankfulness and the true spirit of Christmas released.

Let the little ones wait on the stairsteps peeking through the bannisters for Santa. Our stairsteps can be memory and scrapbooks filled to overflowing. Time together or notes to distant ones that abound with inner sharing are the most precious gifts.

Dear reader, please enjoy these thoughts just for your heart.

DECEMBER 5

The house is silent, and even the end-table dust isn't moving. The quiet of night is shared with the high moving stars passing from hemisphere to hemisphere, from dark to light and back again. Catch this peace that is available through the miracle of life's blessings. Feel this rotating energy in your own circle of space today.

Gazing out my window from the gradually lightening house, I saw the Spirit of Christmas sweep by in a gentle cloud of fog. It held to the treetops like a blanket of winter's comfort while the earth beneath yawned clearly in view. The tree roots stretched in early morning wakefulness. Roots of thought are buried deeper. I look forward to finding more evidences of this season with you.

But for now, I thank you for thinking about this. I'm going back to sleep a while longer. It's still too early, and I had gotten up ahead of the alarm clock.

Thirty minutes later, I'm up, and the sun has broken through. In its glow and warmth, I hear a whispered message: Give *time* a big space on your list of gifts.

Pure blue sky is pushing away the foggy clouds, and an airliner is leaving a trail of excitement for its happy passengers. Ah! Traveling into the blue is such a fun thought! What a gift that would be!

Sunshine pours through my windows now, and our day is warming. The Sago palm is bending its four long new fronds. I wonder how far these can reach?

Oh, yes, I dusted the furniture because the pastor is coming for tea and mini-muffins this afternoon. Visiting and accepting invitations are such gracious gifts of the season!

Welcome to your new day!

DECEMBER 6

December 6th has arrived, and it has brought yesterday's memories in gift wrappings. I ponder these in bed as I awaken from a good sleep. Do you ever celebrate when the blessings of sleep have refreshed you for eight hours without sleep therapy required? Already I am anticipating the joy of a spirit-filled afternoon of talking and the e-mail joy of laughing without anyone hearing me. So, celebrating with not one, but two, pieces of cinnamon toast and a cup of microwaved coffee brings today's increasing daylight a little nearer the shutters' opening. You see, these are delightful folding shutters on my window that give upturned, slow sips of day, even a rainy day such as this. Yes, we can drink in the Spirit of Christmas with our coffee in delicate moments of reverence. Truly this is another, "Good Morning!"

It's now a homespun day. I'm making homemade potato soup and listening to the raindrops play their own music against the window screens. This kind of day is cherished just for being here.

So, while my old purple bathrobe provides warming comfort and the thoughts of the crock pot giving new aromas later, I bring the little neglected lists into completion. Calendars, addresses and dear friends are going right along into the New Year with a fresh start in recording all the changes. This will be a way of taking the Christmas Spirit over the threshold into the next year of dreams. Please join in if you have the time or put this in your soon-to-do moments.

Right now, this author is going to settle into the arm chair and reflect on what new adventures are waiting beyond my winter garden and gate. Life always holds gateways for exploring. When the sun comes out, maybe I will take a walk through a colonial winter garden in Williamsburg and pass through another gate that graces a beautiful white picket fence. I really like picket fences, always so welcoming with their little pointed tops. These have held picturesque history in silence through decades. Wouldn't it have been wonderful if someone had made long-ago-audio recordings near these fences? Would we hear horses' hooves on the gravel and historical voices that anticipate our place in time? In listening, would we hear the grunts of strength behind the mortar, brick and stones being placed? The wreaths on the Christmas doors back then are also seen today, bringing our time back into focus. I love to imagine these things. Thank you for this indulgence!

The Christmas Spirit is gliding on the wings of the birds and settling gently in the tree tops to sway in the seasonal breezes. Let's go and find where else we might find the spirit moving through the day. Do you hear the melody playing as if to put a musical signature on the day? Perhaps you may find a couple of alone moments when inspiration touches the inner you. These only come in quiet invitation from your heart, but, with inspiration, we soar into the season of discovery. You will have your own gift of inspiration to be unwrapped, allowing the flowing wings of dreams.

Yes, the Spirit of Christmas can be dreams that elevate you to new realms.

Let's leave this page open. Something new is going to pop up!

Something simple is reaching out to shake a hand extended and hearing the receiver say, "Your hand is so warm!" This is another little gift of warmth supplied without any directed intention. Just that welcoming to a friend leads us to discover that warmth is given and found within the Spirit of Christmas and will not disappear after the season has departed. Warmth doesn't have to come from the fireplace with burning logs. It can prevail in the warmth of touch and smile. Hello to another little free expression of thoughtfulness!

3:21 p.m. seems to be a countdown to moving on.

The rain continues to make its wants known. Here's a little thought to ponder: Have you ever treated yourself like a guest visiting in your home? Now don't scowl, because it can be a wonderful acknowledgement of your own hospitality skills. Fix the beverage of your choice, and grab goodies that probably are already waiting in the cookie jar. Get a napkin, sit down in your favorite chosen spot and savor the quiet for a moment. Turn on the music and just be entertained like a special person. Because you are! Now way back in the military-social protocol days, it was proper to make a social call in and out in just 20 minutes. So, in your own home, you can laugh and say, "Are you serious?" Yes, serious, and you can devote at least 20 minutes to yourself. Begin to recognize that the spirit of fun is very important.

Dream lists come rarely; however, they are not to be ignored. In dreaming up the design for my new business card after the publication of *Power Steering 2*, I had to come up with concepts for both the front and back. It was a hop-out-of-bed-and-race-to-follow the easy design. It was conceived and requested in an email with the ordering of "when it is convenient." This isn't the season to pile more work on the marketing department. My only requirement was to purchase these colorful and informative cards in time to spread silently the Christmas Spirit of giving. We can say with amazement that our brain output can be an unexpected surprise. Thank you, Lord, for this little nudge for the continuance of spirit-filled happiness.

It is now six hours later on the wings of time.

These wings of time led to a storage area that brought a trembling moment. There, walking in the distance toward me, was this beautiful angel dressed in a long brown coat that covered what I felt must be her winged feet. Her long golden-blonde hair glistened. I had been anxious and fearful about going up the many steps and past great numbers of closed storage doors. But the angel gave a warm greeting and lovely smile as she approached, and my fears fell away. I shared with her my anxieties, and she offered to go along with me. I declined, because I knew that her day would have many others to calm with the warmth of holiday cheer.

The key fit the lock, and, rolling up the metal door, I immediately saw some of the Christmas decorations ready to come home, especially, the strand of stars to hang lit up along the patio fence.

My time in the storage unit became a special occasion. I found an original painting, one-of-a kind, painted by a one-of-a kind artist who is watching from a heavenly branch. He painted it long ago with one hand while recuperating from surgery. I wanted to jump in the snow drifts in his skilled painting artistry of Christmas trees.

But, whoa! It was accidentally left quite unnoticed, until back home I saw that there was something missing. Quick, go back! I found it standing just where it had been left - beside the elevator. Elevated thankfulness rose from my lips and heart.

On the errands-to-do came the need to finish the grocery list due to my shelves emptying during the past busy month. In departing the store, I stopped and called to a familiar cashier and wished her a Merry

Christmas. She waved a little warm miracle across the huge box store.

There followed the usual packing the plastic bags into the car and then the careful execution of a right turn. On my way! That right turn became the right place and time. Look! There standing, a little bent, was a blue spruce in a red container. Perfect for my needs. I stopped and called across the street to the gentlemen who was guarding my cherished tree.

"Yes, it's for sale, and it is a blue spruce."

"Oooh, save it and I'll drive right over!"

Then the purchase, and he placed it on the floor in front of the front seat. Miraculously, it fit, helped by the bend of its head just a little. Now the passenger area was well filled with my beautiful tree like silent night before rising light. How on earth was I going to get this up onto the patio?

A miraculous idea arrived, several phone calls were made, and one resulted to accomplish the need in filling.

"Yes, I'll give you a phone number, and you can call our maintenance man."

Then, within forty-five minutes, little Blue was riding in a cart in elegant fashion from my car to the patio up steep steps. Now it resides on the patio in view of the entry window for great admiration.

Christmas Spirit keeps enveloping the day. The company maintenance man said, "No charge, just Merry Christmas." I put one of my author cards in his helping hand and a little tip, too.

Moments later, a cheery voice graced my phone. We will meet next week. She loves Christmas, too, and she is eager to read our efforts to capture the essence of holiday Spirit. She's another angel because of all she does for everyone without one word of complaint. Currently, she's working to assist her mother in the healing process from a 24/7 need. The wings of time will deliver to them both an invitation to tea soon.

Dear reader, we are discovering that the Spirit of Christmas is alive, and we need to keep recognizing and encouraging it.

In the closing moments of today, the holding of hands around the dinner table led to another miracle of love. My family recounted blessings that meant the Spirit of Christmas had been a constant visitor. Listening to the story of my daughter's two trips to the Emergency Room and her care in the hands of the workers there, I clasped my hands in preparation for prayer. It was a surprise case of supraventricular tachycardia (SVT). That's a rhythm of the heart that is beating much too fast. Seven medical angels brought her back to a slower pace. Feeling the Spirit of Christmas around us, I prayerfully bowed my head in gratitude.

"Thank you, Father, from this mother's heart." Could we possibly fathom the words inside the heart of Christ's mother or her strength when, in the end, she held timeless history in her arms?

The day closes with one last bedtime viewing of the computer screen. Tonight, great photography honored an historical tree that has endured over 3200 years. The magnificence of the Redwood reached an accord with the cameras. This is a miracle of rooted life, and I think about my little blue spruce which has found a Christmas home.

Savored feelings are invisible, yet they define the roots within our hearts and stretch forth for sharing. This insight is a prayer for me.

Amen.

DECEMBER 7

It's an evening with warming thoughts of a grocery store moment. It's where you bring your own bag, fill it, unpack it at the register, pay and re-bag it for the homeward trip. This makes the purchases feel more personal. But I am remembering a moment when someone dressed in a black and white gown and a white scarf caught the side of my eye. I turned and saw this elegant and tall lady who wore a solemn expression. Slowly, I reached into my purse and handed her one of my author cards with the three postage-sized, colorful book covers.

"Here, these are inspirational books, and you may like these!" She smiled, and I handed her another for her companion, who was also in the garb of a mission. Maybe now, in thinking back to the scene, I realize that she may have been from a distant monastery. Somewhere out there, great fruitcakes are created. This evening thought creates a warm vision of heart that lets me see that this was the Spirit of Christmas smiling. You never know where it will reveal itself before moving on in its winged journey.

DECEMBER 8

Early morning, computer and television on. Touching buttons, keys and the heart. The television remote reduced the volume so that the senses would not awaken too abruptly. The television played the music stations and scrolled words explaining songs and performers. But the digital marketing flowed right into my mind and heart when it gently produced words of the season, like, "Thankful" and "Blessings." The final screen acknowledged the Spirit of Christmas. The Spirit was silent, but the word "Christmas" was a christening for the season. God and morning have etched the season with another touch of beauty.

If you, the reader, have many other readings and errands and want to scroll to the last recording of music, that's fine. You can get way into the month yet to be traveled. But this writer will just wait for other surprise appearances of Christmas Spirit day by day. It will be hard to pick just one favorite demonstration.

The Memory Bank is quickly filling with the joyous things I see beyond my front door. Have you looked at the tree tops and noticed some small to large baskets of greenery and wondered what Southern charm is so tall? These are rare, but I am seeing large clusters of mistletoe cherished by florists in two tree tops in my neighborhood. The old eighteenth-century custom was for the hunters to shoot these out of their quiet solitude and bring them home with the prized deer. So, if you are fortunate to be in such a doorway of Christmas, just let it be the best present you could ever wish to receive.

On to the pharmacy to be greeted with the friendly smiles and helpfulness of the staff. Let's toss that one in our large bag of received gifts. The ride to the post office resulted in numerous catalogs competing for household space in hopes that the shopping hasn't been completed yet. Free shipping is another distraction, too. The notice in the box says, "Priority Mail." It's a suggestion that a big box is in the back awaiting a key to release its captivity. Let's go see what has been packed.

Oh! It looks like a pregnant zebra. Ha! Don't say, "The author is impossible in describing sights and sounds." Truly, the zebra is about to give birth to a kicking bit of surprise. Do you get a kick out of surprises? That's the kid in all of us! Being childlike is an essential sensitivity in appreciating this season of Christmas Spirit.

The bank teller shared that she and her children are all set for the holidays and that they were going over to the Eastern Shore for their family Christmas. I queried whether it will be an old-fashioned Christmas?

"Oh, my, yes! The house will be displayed in all the old-fashioned antique adornments, and the feast will be Grandma's and Mother's touches of artistry, tasting treats and delicious aromas exuding from the kitchen."

That sounds like a Norman Rockwell holiday, all picture perfect! Don't you just wish we could ride across the Chesapeake Bay Bridge and be the silent party of crashing photographers?

The drive time home did not waste one minute before the exit to my home appeared. I was feeling happy. Waves of joy penetrating life - isn't this what we all need?

Adventure is spice for life. Thankfulness is my afternoon sip of tea and slow bites of mini-muffins. While the house fills with music, I go in search of the scissors to open this giant box of loving packaging that I received from my sister. Get ready! Excitement might raise the blood pressure, but it can be allowed momentarily for surprises. This is a once-a-year capture of the Spirit of Christmas! Tranquility will arrive later.

A crimson and purple sunset fills the sky outside my three windows of view, and I bring the box upstairs as the lavender-pink of evening defines the last heart-throbbing moments of day in my living room. The box had arrived from an early elf delivery, and now I have it open to find the light-emitting LED candles and tiny

Christmas figurines given life by batteries. It's a dizzying delight to unwrap all of these small treasures. There are also emergency flashlights, other ornaments and a nutcracker. I see a pale moon outside waiting for the dark of sky. So, candles for lighting up the world with a blend of moonlight create a romantic, magical scene in my living room! I feel in touch with the beauty of life. Let's label today, "beautiful."

Time now for a phone call to tell my sister how very special, generous and thoughtful she always is. At first, the flight of my enthused, inner zebra got cut short by the phone circuits going dead. There is adequate zoo feed, but the across-the-mountains phone service might have been stopped cold by a winter storm. But, finally, the connection!

After abundant chatter about the little candle cherubs, tree decorations and table LED candles that light on four-hour shifts, I discovered that while my sister was on her cell phone, she was baking cookies. I thought I had smelled them! We always have so much fun talking and adding smiles across the miles.

Returning to the computer screen from a forty-six-minute cessation, I found a LinkedIn friend whom I remembered from our art studio days when we both were also teaching. It's wonderful that the Spirit of Christmas keeps springing long-ago memories to freedom in a now-reality again.

Silence and meditation can help these memories find new life. I put myself in a deep tranquility, and I notice smells. The fragrances of the season rise to envelop me - freshly cut sage, rosemary and the smoking embers of a campfire. I detect the faint odors of the colonial crescents from the night before.

The power of fragrances to bring memories alive in the current moment first caught my attention through a gentleman's pipe resting on the lips of story-telling. I was transported into a long-ago entering of a New England general store and seeing chairs around a pot -bellied stove, and I wondered about their old-age sharing. A pickle barrel not too far away hefted a tangy vinegar and salt fragrance. I found myself walking past the fudge and wishing for a piece of taffy. These are remnants of a time when maple sugar hayrides left tracks through the wintery snow. These little memory snapshots are like the Currier & Ives pictures that are framed ubiquitously in antique stores. I see rough-hewn logs waiting to be used and the heavy wrinkled hands that had worked the snow drifts of winter amid dreams of lazy chairs on distant tropical beaches. Fragrances evoked these pieces of life goodness. Sharing these old scenes with you puts us in the spirit of the season.

Just a little mistletoe above the door of memory as we move closer to the early morning hours of a new day. This time taken to observe deep roots in the soil and then tunneling deeper for the warmth of remembrances sensitize this author's emotions. Have any of these little recollections given your shoulders a lift? The Spirit of Christmas surrounds us, and we can keep it alive month after month until the light of the high star in December gives witness to the greatest wonder of earth. Memories and stories are gifts that can be transmitted from lips to printed or digital pages. Our culture is accustomed to the latter now. Memories get pieced back into stories, big balls of yarn ready for spinning into a rug of beautiful design. Maybe Aladdin's rug got caught on the weather highs and will flop in front of us by a dying wind! Let's go! Or, if your mood is calmer, wrap yourself in the quiet comfort that words cannot explain. You receive feelings brought into awareness from your seasons of need. Time is so precious! Staying tuned is to put the vehicle of yourself in the service station. Plug into the Spirit of Christmas that is around you. It is electric with abounding and astounding energy. Each one of your days is personal. When you have found these cherished feelings, then angels must be singing. Take deep breaths and fall into the reflections of memory. There lies great contentment. This author won't accompany you on your journey, because her own is here in front of her eyes. Aware, I listen to sounds in a complete tuning to what I normally tune out. Now here come the mystical, magical, breath-stealing gifts that cause the heart to beat quicker.

It is almost time to close the day. Just a little mending needs to be done first. I'll go find a spool of thread to restore appropriate dressing. As we thread our way through these golden days of the Christmas season, we remember the totality of small things that compose the spirit's fabric. It's not just pine needles that provide all the essence of the season. Oh, how I love my blue spruce in its holiday dressing! A gold star on top adorned by a big red ribbon and a red bell hanging quietly. In past days, old-fashioned bells would have livened the horses' harnesses. I wonder if the donkeys and camels of long ago would have been dressed in blankets and bells? Just a wandering thought as the nighttime winter wind caresses the door and I drift into the profundity of peaceful sleep.

DECEMBER 9.

We have just scrolled by yesterday. High in the night sky, a planet was climbing to its own orbital heights. In meditative moments, I measured a bright star moving from one window pane to another in an ascending arc. Just the little things that add brilliance to our time. What small significance can my presence bring to someone today?

Lifting the load for my editor and publisher is the last order of business in today's stream of work. Sending a holiday message that the next publishing book can wait in the incubation stage a while longer. Dear reader, it's important that the Spirit of Christmas thrives without the demands of hurry. My little message is just a little gift for the publisher's desk, which is always toiling in dedication to clients.

DECEMBER 11

This morning has taken on a new day, new sunrise and time to create a sky-view masterpiece. During uncounted sunrises, I have taken thousands of pictures. They are always miracles caught for later review. The shadows of this morning haven't even been fanned by a breeze. I am outside to take photos and then back inside to admire with awe the Master Artist's work. Our Great Creator allows us to be true witnesses to the glory, power and the spirit that abound beyond the holidays. It's the Light of the World to feel, to see and to love. Sunrise!

Now with this experience, we feel the truth of the birth of Christ to be the light for our souls. In whatever faith you live, it all belongs on the heavenward ascent. Seeing the beauty of life and acknowledging its presence are the first steps in the trek toward "peace on earth and goodwill to mankind."

In retrospect, the very soul of today was in waking early before the sunrise. Numbers, numbers, and numbers of pictures were taken as the shore of the east coast in the USA awoke to Sunday. I prepared inside, went outside, got very cold for several pictures, re-warmed inside, and then went out again for more. My series of the waking sun shows the delightful palette of crimson, rose and golden hues of sky against which the silhouetted trees branch their shapes. The rise of colors widened and later faded into a scope of blue. Back inside, I just couldn't capture it all through my trio of windows. This time of taking perhaps 100 shots came quickly, easily, and joyfully. To this author and photographer, it was a giant explosion of the Spirit of the Christmas sky and I was there as witness and capturer.

If you slept through this miracle of colors, I will gladly share with you this beginning of Sun Day. The miracles of sky continue to unfold for the many holiday travelers taking to the airways. Streaks climbing, criss-crossed con-trails piercing the sky, thin white arrows honing on their destinations. I captured a photo of a spectacular one that formed a half-circle in descent from high altitudes, seeking a landing out there somewhere. The day began with such emotion that the fountain burst forth and spit a crystal edging around the pond. Now you have shared in my blessings of a southern-winter wonder.

It reminds me of snow on the roads. May all the stranding highways melt their snow quickly throughout the country. I recall being marooned with two wee ones and a very hungry cat for thirteen hours once upon a time, and I had no food except Snicker's candy bars. We had missed the exit from the main highway, and there was no turn-around possibility like the airplane this morning had in the lane-less freedom of the sky. Even the helicopters that passed above us seemed to mark their thoughts with, "We don't know what to do for them."

Ah, but there's a pot of beef stew in the crock pot that in six or seven hours will greet our destination of hunger with a big helping of potatoes, carrots, celery and, of course, the purple onion. There's still time to join in if you like old-fashioned cooking and hot biscuits. Well, to be honest, unless there is company, the biscuits will still be waiting on the refrigerator shelf. Home is so comfortable today, now that the new maroon sofa and coffee table have reached my address. Yes, that's another sliver of contentment slipping on to this page.

Would you believe that playing dress-up back when still holds amusement today? Hmm, maybe you aren't afraid to admit to childish creative spurts? Back in the spring months, I spied little planter holders on wheels. These were intriguing, but I didn't know when I could use them.

I bought three, and then I deposited them in waiting mode in the trunk of my car. Weeks later, after my big move to this new apartment, I gave them residence in the cloak closet. Off we go! In needing more seating space around the new coffee table, I wondered, "Can the planters serve as basic seating if I add pillows?" So, out of the closet and up the stairs I brought them. When taking off the descriptive labels, I had a pleasant surprise. The casters could be locked! So, with trial and error and a bit of humor, I put different pillows on one and then sat at the coffee table (without the coffee however.)

Sure enough, the wild creative idea worked. So, the casters are locked, and now these are waiting for three pillows for modern Seiza, my adaptation of Japanese seating on the floor. Then I jump to the sofa to admire the new additions. Wow! My trio of windows reflect in the glass coffee table a sharing of the sky that seems a reversal of the universe far beyond our tiny planet. The miracle of this Sunday just keeps deepening.

Hello! It's later. It's still December 11, and I have made trips into town. On the way back from errands, I saw two sun dogs. Now these won't get descriptive kennel names, and they weren't barking in their high kennel sky. However, they certainly were an indication that the weather is changing and will become colder. As you have already surmised, I love to watch the clouds, and I could fill a photographic portfolio of these cosmic beauties. Maybe it's that I have my head in the clouds and find that these have all kinds of moods. Just a little touch of psychology in the heart! Don't you love the freedom of the sky? The Spirit of Christmas is always there, drifting in clouds and colors, caught in dreamland.

While we have been searching for the Spirit of Christmas, I just found one of these miracles right here in my own home! If a sneeze is for one instant heart-stopping, then we are lucky to have sneezes of surprises, just like now. I had a phone call from family that they are coming for an early Christmas dinner here. I feel happy.

Returning to pillows, permit me to explain why they are so magical to me. As I was leaning on a pillow against the arm of the new sofa, I tossed it off as being a little too bulky. Sliding down the rolled arm of the sofa, I recalled the sofa that was in the lovely country Victorian home of my childhood. Pillows there were just to be plumped every morning on the beds, and there never were any lying on the living room floor or sofa, nor in the big bay windows of the parlor where our piano graced the room. But now there is pillow freedom! They can go anywhere! So, with a big, "Wow," I acknowledge why I love decorator pillows. Sorry if I've bored you with pillow talk and my small personal miracle. But I think by now you understand. Large happiness can reside in small places of the heart.

The Christmas music is now surround-sounding the living room. I'll return to the embrace of the curved arm of my waiting soft sofa.

Thank you, Lord, for a perfect day.

DECEMBER 12

Today is December 12, and it is a straight-line rain event. The forecasters were right, and, hopefully, the stratosphere will warm the freezing elements far above and just keep raindrops watering little Blue Spruce. I'm going to open the First Day of Christmas and allow the "Partridge in a Pear Tree" to fly. The legend comes from a memory game with a storyline recreated from troubadours in medieval times. I am examining my treasure, noting first the dance by a maiden in merry old England and then finding a barcode that has a label of "Twelve Days of Dickens Village." It is produced in porcelain with a hand-painted design in "Department 56." In looking for the artist that hand painted these gems and a production date, I have concluded that no price tag can measure the history of these pieces from memory's time. I also have no date when I purchased this cherished beginning set of legends, but, no matter. We'll just start today and roll toward tomorrow. Just remember that these are priceless in another of my Spirit of

Christmas proclamations. Let's continue in our overflowing cup up of joy. (Sorry, it is only 9:15 a.m. and I am this enthusiastic already even with no eggnog yet!)

Fourteen hours later, and I am returning to write before the day closes out. I want to share this particular viewpoint:

The evening full moon slowly rose after 5:00 p.m., and my camera and I began taking pictures. When outside became too cold and only the airliner con-trails were wending their way high aloft, I came inside. The twilight began to wane, and the moon played hide and seek in the trees beyond. "Just one more picture to capture the beauty of God's mystery," I said to myself. I took one last shot through the middle window pane. It looked pretty dark along the vertical reach of the lens, but the full moon has its own majesty shining. Then, later in the last few minutes of today, I returned to look at the photo, but this time with the computer view. I discovered that looking straight ahead at the screen, my eyes took in much framing of the night encroaching

69

upon the moon. However, looking at 45 degrees presented a totally different angling of light from the right and the left. Tomorrow, I'll take it to the studio and have a copy made in order to preserve that touch of Christmas Spirit from the lens to canvas. As I tried to print it on paper tonight, would you believe that the printer ink announced that it had first dibs on my time, and it definitely wants a new breakfast cartridge?

Now the cold of night beyond my window and the warmth of comfort inside render me half asleep. I look forward to continuing with you tomorrow. Good night!

DECEMBER 13

December 13 opens its heart to the new day, and with it, we see the sunrise smiling, too. Happiness is attaching to the season like the garlands holding onto the staircase and the stars illuminating the walkway. If these thoughts had been denied, it would be the sin of my lack of gratefulness. Too often we push aside the inner illuminations of the Master. The day outside is already singing praises to Him. We will walk our own pace on our path on this planet of destiny. It is the second of the twelve days of Christmas. Let's go and lift the contents from the box that housed it for a long time.

The day has taken its own course. The "two turtle doves" in the song lyrics have escaped the pretty green nest that they were supposed to be in. So, we shall enjoy two little Christmas trees and a bird house that they may have flown to. On my porcelain tableau, the English lady has a shawl around her shoulders and holds the hand of the little girl with the small basket of bird seed. Traditions like the two turtle doves so quickly fly away and are recalled now and then in a familiar song. Their history is only a little story from the merry old England in the far-off past.

Today, a friend shared the story of Scrooge that Charles Dickens made famous, and it returns each Christmas season to remind us of the Spirit of Christmas. Are there Scrooges still hovering in the unnoticed wings who need a touch of caring? Let's be the hearts that can bear the loss of Christmas spirit for others and walk with those besieged by the Scrooges of modern times. Perhaps the two doves will return gently to their roosting place with soft titters and cooing.

Today opened with brush strokes like the dry sweeps of a Japanese artist's thoughts. The day has worn so many miles. I am glad to return to home where music reverberates against the walls and makes the room cozier. I'll bid a goodnight and allow the world to continue its orbital spin. This passenger can do no more.

Tonight, my hopes are pinned to a poster that features the moonrise over the Atlantic Ocean and my book cover of *Time on the Turn*.

Yes, it will land on a wall in a big book exposition in London and will share from within its book spine descriptions of the old-fashioned American life and history in the thumbnail sketches which I authored.

You can't fathom some of the hefty words that describe the Spirit of Christmas unless you have lived them. This afternoon brought a glass of eggnog and a raspberry torte adorning a holiday plate on which a red cardinal was singing. Over this plate of happiness and the sharing of life experiences with someone, a new word formed within the lining of my heart: Harmony. It has reached a pure beat with others. Certainly, this harmony must have also been felt by the stable witnesses of man and beast centuries ago in old Bethlehem.

There's a new page to be opened in the discovery of harmony. It's more than an emotion. It is an anchoring and a throw of a life preserver to others in choppy waters. Sometimes all that is required to harmonize with someone else is an encouraging touch of urging and caring. Good night!

DECEMBER 16

The date line indicates December 16, and from this vantage point, the skies are seeking a relief of winter wind and chill. The word that comes to mind is "cathedral," and this is limitless. I feel the surging of joy that the sky is the limit, and I dance. The ceilings of home make cathedrals, too.

Through the windows of my cathedral, I see that the tall tree-like shrubbery is getting a crowning glory of a season's growth. Everything outside looks manicured, and the orange and yellow tulips planted are still in springtime waiting to emerge with, Hello!" If you know your own cathedrals of life, you can feel this refreshing sense of leaving the old year behind and the newness soon to break into celebration. Cathedrals first imposed themselves in my awareness of the solid structuring of the Old World. What enchantment! The paintings that burst from pages of the art history collections stirred my soul. I gained a new feeling of living in the great cathedral of the world at large. I am not talking of great stone structures like the House of Representatives, but just the simple and light framework of sunrises, sunsets and the stars of night. There's majesty and greatness surrounding our every breath of life. Look at where you have come, how far, and the freedom you have to understand precious concepts in new and more meaningful ways. Cathedral, I must remember to watch for your signs more often.

"Thank you, Father!"

We don't consider ourselves slow learners; however, special moments sometimes are hard to describe. Today our chosen word befitting the Spirit of Christmas is "blessings." Where blessings enter your life and mine are probably very different, but we cherish these elusive gifts. My first understanding of blessings came as a child around the large rectangular table in the kitchen filled with homemade delights. The "blessing" was said with all hands holding, and I wondered if the holding tight meant so it wouldn't dash away? Then there was a long-drawn-out blessing in the church pews that got awfully hard to sit through. The sermons seemed to be endless, and there seemed to be some hell-fire statements too. Was there something cooking that I didn't understand?

But now, with experience and a larger world view, I consider the wonder of blessings with reverence for this word. It comes with underpinnings of riches such as comfort, peace and love. Blessings abound at Christmas. The season of Christmas brings enlightenment. Light from candles produce gentle moments when soft prayers can be shared and savored and allowed to fill the heart. There are no sermonettes for blessings that do justice, because they are sometimes too subtle for adequate description. They can be present around us, but we just may be too busy to notice. When we transform ourselves into lights for the world, our ability to recognize blessings becomes stronger. By shining on them and illustrating them to others, we can fill the world with hope. Hope is a natural by-product of blessings.

Hope fills the hearts, minds and souls of people and seeds dreams. Hope and dreams have been responsible for the construction of great edifices from the time of creative planning to the finishing touches of a skyscraper, space station or cathedral. So high, this truth of hope! It can accompany us on all our journeys. For tonight, grateful for blessings and the hope I feel, I am going to allow the season to reign in quiet and peace, brought to me by my new recipe for filling heart and soul.

I will prepare for sleep by listening to music. The rhythm of music in whatever culture moves from the instrumentalists and vocalists to the ears of the grateful listener. There's an after-glow of emotions when the concert has passed its climax. Watching the concert tonight, I burned with mounting excitement. The audience of this concert performance at Lincoln Center rose in unison at the end in appreciation to recognize and honor the performers. This brought great joy to me.

Their standing showed me that this cultural protocol hasn't died. It was a wonderful way to end another day of Christmas Spirit.

DECEMBER 17

Good morning, after four hours of sleep and the opening of a new day with mist beyond the louvers of my windows! Watching the tiny raindrops join into a mist that now is forming a mix of thin snow. As the mighty forces of nature fight with one another, the temperature drops, and the ground outside my home forms a film of black ice.

It is now pouring forth, and the ice will soon be thin frosting on the pine branches. As romantics, we could think of it as nature decorating, but, as realists, it must be reckoned with as a wild and dangerous highway from aloft. Gusts of wind are pouring the storm faster like flour for thickening. The straight little raindrop arrows have become ice blades darting into the earth in diagonal patterns. Whiffs of ice clouds strike the lampposts outside. This has become a powerful force that may bring our little mecca of a town to its knees. No, not by snow drifts, but by the breath of icy strength. The winter artistry is breaking my fast without food, but I savor the entwining of tea flavors in a small cup.

Cups of blessings for us to stop and appreciate the creative strength of the visual and the invisible. Warming thoughts and the surroundings of home that are bringing this author comfort. I hope you have found a night of rest and are prepared to walk slowly today until temperatures climb and the rays of heaven's sun takes front stage. Eyelids are beginning to bow as courtesy, and respect is given to the power of Winter. May the sleet not deliver any emergency needs. My prayer fans from thought to lips and on to the listening of heavenly power. There are no power outages in heaven, only starlight in radiant beams. So, put on your ski togs, and, when the time is right, carefully open the door and venture outside for a slide on a giant frisbee.

Ah, but I am hearing a calling tone. The Spirit of Christmas can arrive with a phone call saying, "I'll stop by with the kids in a little bit." There, ringing the doorbell, were three big smiles and greetings of welcome. Visiting family and friends is so delightful. Do you take time to do this favor to yourself and others? The children were off to a big cookie party, and this author went back to baking teacakes. The kitchen had not yet culminated in the old-fashioned aromas coming from the oven, but I grabbed the best moments taking the pictures of the young ones while their favorite escort, Grandpa, fixed my printer. Then with hugs and handshakes, we promised to learn to play chess sometime soon. My set of dramatic figures of the Civil War are a collector's owning but have never been the subject of learning. There should be always time to learn more about history and life.

Moose Munch and Russian teacakes popped into the mouth make a holiday bite a new taste discovery. The teacakes needed a kick, and the moose gave it just that. If I've infringed on anyone's patented wording, please pardon the reference, but these are the best! How's that for advertising? (That word, "advertising," suggests massive sales. I prefer to window shop, order from catalogs and dodge the lines in the stores.)

Tonight, I'm reading a book brought to me earlier today, and since I wrap my reading around words and events, I'm feeling a strong urge to continue our search for the Spirit of Christmas. Maybe we can go to a plantation out on the James River and learn how the eighteenth and nineteenth centuries' Christmases were celebrated?

At Berkeley Plantation, I have a favorite place to sit in a gazebo and wonder what Mr. Lincoln felt when he reviewed the troops once at this location. Out on a knoll is where "Taps" was composed. Once, I sat on a big stone with the plantation's current owner, and he shared his winged joys of this place. He said, "This is where I'll spend my heaven time now and also in the after time." Mac is a wonderful and generous southern gentleman who swept brides off their feet in the grass and took them through the gazebo door.

Eyelids are bowing again, but this time from sleepy reading. I bid you a goodnight as we tick one more day closer to Christmas!

DECEMBER 18

This is the dawn of Sunday before Christmas, and let's gently explore our personal beginning. We have ventured out to the world of the many surface expressions of the visible Spirit of Christmas. Let's wrap all of these mini-discoveries with a ribbon and package a gift for our own hearts. In searching for the Christmas spirit, we have developed a sense of purpose and have discovered that our adventure is enriched through sharing.

Last night, during a wonderful television sermon, I had an insight that Advent is an adventure with true meaning. That understanding suddenly made a lot of sense to me. Somewhere in the heartlands of sermons, I had missed the origin of Advent. Wow! The idea of Advent as an adventure struck me in an intuitive way, and I discuss the power of intuition in depth in my *Power Steering* books. This insight is a key suggestion to me for more Power Steering. Perhaps this engine of thought should cruise slowly through this great season and take us to the places where we enjoy the gifts of family, friends, fellowship, homespun fun and good food. I remember my son-in-law's suggestion and how happy my family is that this year we are sharing gifts not in boxes to be placed under a cut tree. Oh, but I do give thanks to the Lord, because, as you know, I do love the live blue spruce tree decorated with ribbons in my home. It is a beauty that is a gift for all.

Writing and thinking about the readers and their reactions create a kind of conversation, one that is offered by the writer sometimes with vulnerability. I imagine your reading eyes reflecting the glow of inner fires that warm your living. This is a warmth that will stay with you during new adventures in the winter days ahead! It is December 18, and I feel like a roasting marshmallow, kind of soft and gooey.

Speaking of that, today, Sunday, was preceded last evening by a soft, candy-colored marshmallow cloud that drifted just above my roof top. There were several cloud banks in higher elevation, but my cloud was a fluffy comforter of peace above my home. This morning, the dawn brought the opening eyes glorious colors. I got up and ventured through some writing thoughts at my computer, but then I found that my physical self was suddenly in need of food and more rest. So, I set the alarm in two hours; no, two and half hours; turned off the alarm and said, "Okay, Lord, if you want me to go to church this morning, then wake me at 9:30 a.m." My goodness, right on target, I awoke and felt great! I hurried to get ready for church, and, would you believe? After yesterday's ice storm, the temperature climbed today to a fantastic 72 degrees! Wonderful! The music of the service and the sermon resounded again with the Spirit of Christmas.

At church, I observed my dear former neighbor and widow arriving alone. So, during the greeting time of, "Peace be with you," I said to the woman spontaneously, "Please come after church, and I'll fix omelets." She smiled in appreciation.

We had a lovely conversation and lunch. Her life in the past several weeks had been lived during her husband's parting time. Perhaps our luncheon helped her to release some pent-up stress. Ahead, she has Christmas travel and family who will open their arms to share their big world of Texas. Her quiet trust in sharing her pain and experiences with me exemplified the Spirit of Christmas. Her husband had been Jewish, so we skipped the ham in the cheese omelets as a respect for all faiths in God. Christmas spirit is universal and sometimes travels under the name of compassion.

DECEMBER 19

The December 19 tray quickly filled with activities and errands. Getting the kitchen ready for family arriving with the promise of their personal catering was a challenge, because they had provided no menu for me to know what was going to be prepared. All I knew is that it would be a surprise dinner delight. Right on the queue of the clock, the door flew open to smiles and arms full of pots, pans and goodies hidden in coolers. This is truly a Christmas that not even the blue spruce could have anticipated. Just plum sheer joy that even included one labeled Kumquat from the family's last Florida adventure. The menu evolved, got baked and became a banquet atop the kitchen counter for easy serving. We won't activate your savory taste buds by peeking into the oven to see the ham and other goodies roasting.

The gift of Christmas planning by my children turned out to be a five-star-ranked dinner time of fun, family, fellowship, friendship and flowers. These were the five "f's of a Masterpiece Theater right in my home.

Looking around the living room as we chatted, I saw that the room looked like a flowering nursery. The summertime basket of Boston Fern had grown to overflowing proportions, and a potted red poinsettia stood over three feet tall looking magnificently seasonal atop the antique teacart.

We found ourselves in the very heart of Christmas Spirit, and the gift of it produced the fruit of, "Let's do this again!" The success of our gathering led to planning another "catered" dinner for thespian friends. I had mentioned that my son-in-law plays Scrooge in multiple shows in Colonial Williamsburg during the Christmas season. What drama and adventure might lie ahead when the thespians arrive, and the First Act will be dining!

Back tracking for a moment, I don't want to forget to mention that Elantra needed a late afternoon snack at the filling station. I had slipped cash in my winter coat pocket along with one of my author cards. The attendant appeared to be from the Middle East. Handing him the cash, I told him to keep the change, and

I gave him my card and said, "And this is for you, Merry Christmas!" To my delight, his face lit up with a big smile, the very first I had seen on him in the months that I have purchased gas there. He responded with, "Oh, thank you!" As I departed, I told him I was an author. For a moment, I believe he had a feeling of belonging. His genuine smile reminded me that little acts of kindness in spirit may lift someone's shoulders or remove the wrinkle of frowns.

"Thank you, Father, for small but special moments caught in the tapestry of living."

DECEMBER 20

As the days wind down to the arrival of Christmas Day, we must not neglect the great joy of Christmas giving across computer screens as well as via postage-stamped cards. Today is December 20, and my friends are sharing baby pictures of new arrivals during the year and words of affection or appreciation that carve into my life. Friends are treasures that are home grown and have a special place alongside family.

Dear ones of near and far, thank you for the strong ties that remain through the years. We just pick up where we left off on the last big hug. Some of those are years in waiting for the return of loved ones to my threshold of security. With a smile, I think that this is truly "Homeland Security." Destiny becomes more vivid towards the end of a long life, better defined but still not concluded. The legacy that we leave to one another can be love, guidance in living happily and forgiveness. My heart now holds the regret that I didn't say more often, "I love you!" I visualize life as a track meet, and suddenly it is my turn to carry the baton. The baton should be a message of joy!

The baton got passed to me a few minutes ago. The words for this book had been flowing like a river, and I saw no rapids ahead. But the rapids came up fast, the temptation to crash and the rationalization of saying, "Just go to sleep, it will all come together another time." Oh, so wrong, it takes will power to bypass this urge and dig your heels into the time of sharing. When I realized I held the baton, I found the strength to finish the section I had started writing.

When capturing the Spirit of Christmas, it's like jumping aboard a train with ticket in hand and ready for the great Conductor to show the shining rails that roll past old landmarks and memories. What a lovely experience on this day of sunny exposure to winter! Landmarks race past your window, and breathless moments return in anticipation of the next stops in your life. It is the right time and the right track.

Sometimes, the typing keys produce insights that surprise me. The one I have right now is this: There is a Spirit of everyday. It is not only the spirit of the Christmas miracle of a great birth that got proclaimed in the far Eastern sky. The four candles of Advent may just as well represent the four seasons of the year. They emit the light that promises, "Peace on earth and goodwill to humankind!" Yes, I used author's license to change the word from "man" to "humankind." That includes the ladies, too!

If the candles of Advent represent markings of time, then time is something of capital importance. Time! Earlier today I was gifted the presence of the elegant charm of a precious friend who gave me some time with her presence. We live in a digital and virtual age. I had the company of a person in time, not an avatar or a Facebook video.

Dear reader, I hope you can feel the energy that is reaching out to all who can perceive happiness. Perfection isn't the masterpiece that we search to attain through toil; rather, it is found in the genuine moments of joy-time. Sitting on the same sofa is true friendship. Take a moment in your life to absorb this gift of time. No price tag sale will ever reward you like these cherished moments.

I can't say why the song comes to me now, "Carry Me Back to Old Virginny," bringing a nostalgic image to mind of a fireplace filled with warmth and charm. Maybe the flames of the Advent candles and their representation of time move me to such imagining. Time continues beyond the four rich blue flames of Advent.

Contentment has been expressed many times in many ways. Do you ever just put this feeling into word phrases? It is experienced when the contents of life are treasures of experience, warm in the safe keeping of the inner soul. It's that frame that holds the work of mind and hands in the sufficiency of peace. Breaths and sighs of excitement reveal that you can just not wait to open the door to the errands and adventures of tomorrow. Then the energy that we expend needs to be repleted. I do this with a power nap. That means a short time-out for doing nothing except to close the eye lids, slow the pulse and brain waves and nod off into private, personal dreamland. One look at the puppy beside you doing this shows you the obvious benefits!

Silent Night - The silence of night has crept to the door of day's fine closing. You didn't hear its entry or the exit even with the ears of quiet contemplation. The surroundings are mystified by its holy presence. It's is like finishing a book's last pages and wishing for one more intriguing story line.

The Silence of Night as it drifted across the Little Town of Bethlehem like fog must have been oh-so-still and profound. It was the holding of audience breath before the heralding of the angels in the opening act. Then came their choruses in the high heavens of stars and milky way clouds. Is it possible to replicate the sights, sounds and feelings of Silent Night within our world today? If this thought crosses your mind, can your heart provide the answer now?

The evening hours tonight marched forth into a quiet time of reflection for me, thinking about the little wisps of peace and satisfaction that today has spent when all was given with no cost at all. It is gone! Waiting now for the Spirit of Christmas to shine again. Can you feel this quest of wonder? Twinkling lights in distant family homes bring a gentle tear to slide slowly down my cheek. The tear is a memory close to the heart and soul of life. It is a little refrain of Silent Night emerging from within you in a glistening liquid. We are part of the silent night without need of armor or shield. We hear the music as praise worthy to be sung to the Messiah, as Handel gave it to the world. Oh, Holy Night, can this be the coming of a second? Or a third? Or a millionth? Just one more soft tear glides slowly across the cheek of earth and me.

The Spirit of Christmas is often locked within the heart of people and fails to become the light of a brand-new day. It is like an unborn baby. But the birth of a new day is heralded in colors before the sunrise reaches its edge of continental light. As the orb of sun slowly etches the sky above the oceans to land in our view, its light for the world begins to pull in and shrink the long shadows. This is the same effect as love, which lights our lives in truth and distinguishes the real from the shadows. Love is the rain that waters in our eyes above a disarming smile from the heart. Love and the spirit of Christmas are the same.

In human form, intangible love became touchable in the person of Christ. This gift from God has been known for 21 centuries, and yet so many have never found the manger of truth. Our search for the Spirit of Christmas is really a search for love so powerful in its simplicity and gentleness that it cannot be contained. It releases and plays forward in a sharing with everyone, like the release of the sun at the dawn of a new day.

This day is closing like my eyes. I drift away, peaceful and moved and happy that you have accompanied me this far on our journey. Good night!

DECEMBER 21

Dare we be so bold as to hold forth hope that the Spirit of Christmas is unmasked and that the reader finds herself surrounded in this calm of personal experience? Today is December 21, but we still have an armful of hours before it has totally arrived.

As we move into the morning, we shouldn't forget the little blessings of the everyday-waking activities. It's wonderful if the early rituals are just thought of as blessings with no medication required to receive them. For the gentlemen, the shaving that hasn't resulted in a bite by the razor is an example of a waking-up activity blessed by an annoyance that did not occur. The old comment by an English professor who said, "Don't you see?" reminds us that seeing is a blessing when the mirror returns a smile at the day's beginning. Seeing also implies insight, as the professor desires for his student. So, today let's focus on blessings and see where this leads.

I was autographing a recent release of *Power Steering 2* for my new physician, and his response to the book surprised me. He leafed through several pages and said, "I like the looks of this. I'm going to read it when I get home tonight!" He questioned my pen name of M. J. Scott when he knows me as Marilyn. I explained that when I first began writing, women authors were not taken seriously always, so I chose a pen name that sounded masculine, but which was not dishonest about my name. "Well, good for you!" he replied. I felt accepted by him on several levels, and that was a blessing for me.

Then stopping at the lawyer's office, and finally having a new shipment of books, I was able to present one to the secretary and friend who exclaimed with excitement, "Oh, I get my very own copy!" This rather massaged the ego, but the best emotions I experienced during my visit came from her describing her grandchildren and their sparkling eyes on Christmas morning. These little life recordings of happiness are blessings that we often let slide by unnoticed.

A new neighbor stopped walking the mini-sized Yorkshire puppy in order to bring my heavy gallon of spring water up the stairway to my living room. We exchanged comments about how our holidays are continuing to blossom. We acknowledged the pleasantness of the temperature, the lovely green grass outside and that we were having a lovely couple of days and not the winter being experienced in so many parts of the country with the suffering of snow and ice. Another blessing!

I went out to go to a shop that enlarges photos and frames them for me. I was thrilled to find there a special young lady, Christine, who has the skill of converting photos into developed perfection. I waved a greeting. She had Christmas cheer painted on her cheeks with beautiful holly leaves and stuck-on red berries. But best of all was her smile framed in auburn tresses. I had brought a picture from the pastor's own photo shoot to be enlarged and put on canvas and framed. Christine and I worked to highlight the rainbow spun above the church. We hugged in joy when it was completed. Had the intuitive not taken me to her location today, all this would have been lost, because tomorrow she has early holidays off. The intuitive is unlocked from our DNA and often leads us to unpredicted blessings that bring joy. I presented Christine another book to fill her shelf of reading time.

Sometimes the intuitive is a delicate thread to be followed, but it pops up at times that seem inopportune, such as when we are tired and do not want to leave the house again. These unseized moments can be lost opportunities. The body physical and the soul of thought sometimes struggle against one another. This time, tiredness didn't win, and the creativity with Christine brought another blessing. Thank you, Father, for strength.

Ah! Someone thought of me and put their intuition on the wireless cells! This resulted in the miracle of a ringing sound in my home. Happy voices are linguistic and artful blessings of communication. It turns out that dear neighbors are coming to visit before leaving on their Christmas holiday travels. If you place friendship on a platter, make sure that it is made of fine gold. There are some neighbors who remain good neighbors through the years wherever we call home. For me today, another miracle of Christmas blessing. It doesn't matter whether we share a glass of eggnog, tea, orange juice or ice water, we will have a toast of cheer in the Spirit of Christmas.

DECEMBER 22

Good Morning to December 22 and the time of 4:22 a.m.!

On our journey through this month, if you feel like we have hit a lot of detours, don't get alarmed! This is just the way our life in this century goes. The little detours from our racing and planning time are often gems of chance that would have never crossed into our foreseeing. Our minds race so fast, many times with random distractions, and the detours cause us to slow our pace in this race of living. Time is the theme of this morning, and, especially, taking moments to think about others who may need a lift in their daily lives. Gifting your time is the most beautiful package that doesn't need wrapping paper or ribbons. Instead, wrap your arms around someone who is dear and give them the gift of being near.

The Spirit of Christmas is not lost on these little detours into other people's lives; rather, it allows us to revitalize friendships. We do not ever have to be alone, although feelings may fool us into believing so. If we see that is the case for someone feeling lonely, then squeeze in the mission to encourage them in their journey. Our journey through this calendar of discovering the grandeur of the Christmas Spirit leads us to reach out and be willing to enter others' lives with wave lengths of energy. There is power in the Spirit of Christmas! Release some of its energy, and it grows in strength.

Listening to carols may inspire the unexercised vocal chords in your throat to join this glorious wavelength of sharing. So, pick out your favorite ones and add zest to the singing of joy! Christmas Day hasn't arrived yet and needs to be announced! I think that the Spirit of Christmas has taken to the stage today, and all the actors and actresses have taken their marks ready to begin. Each has brought their gifts and talents with laughter, patience and joy.

Look! We have slowed the racing. Being at the right place and right time is the curtain call for the day. We will have large awareness that the unexpected may give us a detour to where we should be.

There at my elbow on the table are the pictures that I am turning into gifts. I had been working at a frantic pace when two arching rainbows, the most brilliant I have ever seen, appeared on my table through the prism of the window nearby. They arrived just when I had completed my dizzying task and left me with the peaceful and certain feeling that I would make it to the medical practice before it closed. I moved at a deliberate pace, and the clock was still ticking with minutes to spare when I opened the door to the practice. I found my doctor and put my gift into his hand while saying, "With lots of love."

For me, I now recognize that giving books is my way of sharing that life in the fast lane should be accompanied by prayers for stoplights of safety. We can manage an extra two minutes to spare. I am sure that heaven will allow us time to manage our witness of earthly creative doing.

I overheard a conversation in which a man was describing his future daughter-in-law. He said, "She's a wholesome girl!" He was speaking genuinely from his heart. Yes, genuineness is another characteristic of the Spirit of Christmas. It is humbling and inspiring and often works silently in the background of us when we recognize this quality in others. While I listened to the conversation, someone graciously invited me to munch from a tray of holiday treats, but, remembering my blood sugar, I declined with the spirit of appreciation. I felt inside a wave of satisfaction. For me, it was another little step in growing up and a blessing towards health.

Dear reader, I could write pages about the heart-to-heart conversation this evening I had over tea with the neighbors who came for their holiday visit before leaving to go see their family in Boston. On the table crowded with nourishments, candles glowed among the pine branches that had been set to cheer the season. Boston awaits them with holiday trimmings and heaping snow on the trees, but these moments first were ours. When they arrived with smiles, hugs and warm coats, we kept the chill of winter beckoning outside the quickly closing door. We sat and talked for hours on the changing mores of society, the times when they were growing up and my recollections of country visits to relatives. Now the relatives are fewer, and friends bring the joy of bonding experiences and the nutrients of laughter.

In a kind act, my neighbor climbed a chair to replace a light bulb and lit the room with caring. In the background, Christmas music played. I felt the day closing with effortless peace and beauty. Now we are prepared for a new day to come. This one has shown us that small blessings are powerful and should be acknowledged with gratitude.

"Thank you, Father, for this time."

DECEMBER 23

Good morning, and the count-down to Christmas is caught on December 23. Through my window, the morning sun is filling the sky and warming the living on earth! A beautiful set of stationary with its reminder of hummingbirds soaring somewhere waits to be opened on my table. Let's wait and see what today will unfold. I'll leave this page open for readiness. Writing is so personal that whoever puts down their thoughts will feel right at home. It doesn't matter the gender.

Last night's teacups, coffee mugs and plates have been washed; the stove surface got a quick sponge rub; laundry got finished; and I am ready for a cup of freshly brewed coffee and a light breakfast. French roast is my current favorite.

Turning on my music channel, the song performed by Bert Kaempfert's orchestra, "I've Gotta' Be Me!" best describes this author's feelings today. Now you know there's always a serious and a humorous side to this author. I'd really like to write another, "T'was the Night

Before Christmas," and all through the house, its quiet, and the puppy is snoozing on top of soft slippers. In the neighborhoods, the wee tikes are taking a last peer through the bannisters at Santa's cookies. The Christmas tree is adorned with tinsel, sparkly lights and a musical chain that is climbing a scale of song. The bells jingle on a carriage pulled by horses bursting with energy. Memories are pinned with ribbons carefully to the needles of my blue spruce pine.

Have you found your own little fireplace of happiness where you can settle a while? Inside my condo, the music is highlighting a piano striking notes in a peaceful melody. I have spent an eternity relaxing, and it's only ten o'clock. My thought about today is that it is a mystery filled with a song without lyrics. I suspect that we will write the lyrics.

Ah, the rewards of saving today just to allow emotions flow with all the Christmas music playing while opening cards with pictures of loved ones inside. These old-fashioned moments are special, and, in return, I'm sending invitations with a picture of my coffee table set for holiday tea. There on the table are sprigs of pine, lit holiday candles and teacup settings. The decision to send my invitations to friends to come soon resulted in an e-mail from a friend in Florida with whom I had wanted to chat. Her G-mail made it feel like it had really happened. Pardon my being so open, but I just feel beamingly happy, and I hope you do, too.

Catching the Christmas Spirit at home on this Friday is a precious happening.

But we mustn't forget the power of the unexpected intuitive. I thought I must call a friend I hadn't heard from in several weeks. While walking to pick up the phone to dial her, it started ringing, and there was her cheery voice. Wow! She had decided to call me in the same moment, so our wavelengths were definitely connected! She had fallen down five brick steps. Ouch! Some stitches helped to mend her elbow.

The song on the music station is playing, "To the End of Time," and it feels so right! I decided it was the right time to make my holiday phone call to my sister in Michigan. So, I dialed, waited, and then began leaving a voice message, "If I'm not interrupting your baking cookies or cakes, do you have time to talk?" She picked up then with her happy voice saying, "Well, do you know, I'm just walking into the kitchen from the freezer with my arms full of cookies and pies for our family gathering on Sunday!" Mmm…I'll let you do your own conjecturing! Then she started giving me recipes over the phone, and it became a drool session. Plus, adding more strands of decorations on my blue spruce while I talked. Oh, happy day! Endless moments that are so dear.

Well, it's now noon time in California, and I'll phone my long-time teacher friend from across-the-patio days and wish her a merry Christmas, too. Suddenly, her heavenly voice answers, and we share family news and holiday stories, and we comment about all the growing up we both have done. Lots to share about the love of our families, and what we both do to nourish our intuitive gifts and passions. Seeing

110

that she is a believer in the intuitive, I will send her copies of *Power Steering* and *Power Steering 2* with joy. Yes, the Spirit of Christmas has reigned not only in my heart today but, also, in the voices of those dear. She reminds me of the time we went to Disney Land with our families and a tiny silver brooch that I had given her years ago. Memories are so cherished.

Thank you, Lord, for this season of connecting lives in a trail of happiness.

Could it be that the intuitive wants to be recognized for its strong sense of direction? I was holding a new glucose meter in my hand and could not get the battery placement situated. While still open, the doorbell rang, and my friends to replace the kitchen ceiling light arrived. I told them I had been thinking about them and that I really needed help in putting the battery in the meter. Done in no time! Proof positive, and now all the little needs have been met. You can form your own conclusions about the intuitive. For me, I just have to try to pay attention to all its subtle nudging.

Have you ever met a Boston Fern in full abundance hanging out on a summer porch or patio? So luxuriant in foliage, but when it comes to joining in with the winter plants, it has a different activity. It sheds like a white cat on a black suit. Well, the greenery turns into little stems of brown, and I just finished being down on my knees whisking up the little leaves. Maybe being down on the knees is good for being thankful. So, I said a prayer of hurry for the little hand vacuum to arrive soon. Now this pruned basket of greenery that loves drinks and space graces the entry hall.

Phone is ringing again! One, two, three rings... Trying to grab the phone before the caller hangs up or goes on recording. What a glorious day of phone calls renewing dear moments and catching up with family and friends! This last call was another prompted by the tea-and-coffee-table picture invitation. They are far away, so I invited them for a summer trip to the Commonwealth of Virginia. Joy permeates the air in like fragrances from a spice rack. I opened the cupboard door, and the fragrance of anise came bursting out of the cookies delivered by last night's guests. Maybe we should add the spices of life so often never mentioned plus tea from the foothills of the Himalayas. Christmas has many portions of wonder. What colors and fragrances describe your happiness?

Music is closing our day with a rhythm of solace to the soul. We have given time to share, we have listened, and we have entered the lives of others for a few moments. Rich experiences packaged and cherished!

Goodnight with sweet dreams where the Spirit of Christmas resides against your cheek and pillow!

DECEMBER 24

Oh, goodness and mercy, this new day of Christmas Eve has brought a new book into the author's surprising life. Will it be a book to read on the coming silent night, or is it the birth of another love story? You see, the birth of Christ is truly a miracle of love for the world's witness beginning twenty-one centuries ago.

In this morning's misty light, it is difficult to realize that the companionship of our daily vignettes of Christmas spirit are passing on. It truly was a new beginning for us, and our searching adventure allowed us to find the birthing of purpose - our own! The Spirit of Christmas is alive and will travel with us into the New Year.

Let's wait and find what this day of Christmas Eve will reveal!

Yes, the social media has been shared from one loving and giving heart this morning to wish the warmth of the holidays to surround all followers. I hope my greetings melt into the crevices of restlessness and bring ease to all who are disquieted. It's just a simple message that someone cares. This miniscule effort of trying to spread the Spirit of Christmas can be exponential thanks to the marvels of social technology. Take a few moments with your good wishes to build upon mine!

I am not seeing many birds outside my window this morning. The joyful bluebirds must be in flight somewhere heading outside this winter zone. But my memory of them has captured their blue songs, and I imagine them in winging flight to celebrate Christmas among the branches of trees farther south.

Ah, the beautiful early Christmas Eve church service with the sparkling angels of children and the young people in their Bethlehem garb reenacting the momentous scene of Christ's birth! The hyper-exuberance of youth and the way they convey messages in pageant are all the beauty of the season, and they make me smile. The music of this evening taxed the vocal chords to joyous release, and this author found her vocal strength had returned for the occasion. The message of the

pastor, the choir of angels lauding the Savior -
the capture of words to express my emotions
about all this fails me. There were all ages in the
pews, but the dear and special children and the
silent, tiny babies watching the pageant unfold
touched me deeply.

When "Silent Night" was softly stirring
hearts, the congregation passed lights from
candle to candle in a growing illumination of
sharing. The light of this time speaks out for
peace on earth. Our hearts were crying from
beauty. Do you feel this Christmas in yours?

The late evening has brought an all-
encompassing-golden fog. It is so beautiful from
my view. It is a gift wrapping of the earth in the
Spirit of Christmas by the Master's hand. The
street lights illuminate the perfection of His
work. I feel the fall of peaceful sleep descending
upon me. I feel you, my co-adventurer in
Christmas Spirit, inside my heart. I wish you
the finest Merry Christmas!

DECEMBER 25

My Christmas greetings to friends and family this year has been the sending of a picture of children of a friend. They are peeking through their grandparents' stairs in the watch for Santa to come and enjoy his cookies. Just a little childlike moment of tenderness and love.

The liturgical calendar extends the Christmas season to January 6, the Feast of the Epiphany. But you and I know that all of us can deliver gifts of Christmas Spirit throughout the entire year. That has been the main discovery of our adventure together.

The best moment of Christmas for me this year is the silent moment of reverence I take for you in joy and gratitude to be part of your life in our season of high hope. I wish you all blessings, and I bequeath you my promise to be inside every share of Christmas Spirit that you deliver. I know that you will be inside mine.

Merry Christmas, good friend!

M. J. Scott

ABOUT THE AUTHOR

Marilyn studied education at Manchester College, earning her B.S. in Education and then her M.A. in Mass Communications at Norfolk State University. She completed all but her dissertation in the doctoral program of Education at California Coast University. A retired gifted-students' teacher who began her career working at Dr. Albert Schweitzer Elementary School in Anaheim, California, Marilyn next devoted 20 years to teaching in the public-school systems of two Virginia cities. Marilyn has also spent years with her own photography business and philanthropic work. In 2015, she became co-founder of The Writer's Council, an organization serving to encourage aspiring writers to achieve their dreams to become published. One of her proudest recognitions is the magazine profile

118

recognition in "Women of Distinction" in 2016.

The author (as M. J. Scott, USA) believes that naming organizations and achievements is a bat of the eye for readers. Much more important, she believes, is the love communicated through genuine sharing of homespun adventures and word-captures of ordinary life. With her characteristic bubbly personality, Marilyn uses humor to connect with readers. This radiates throughout *Finding the Spirit of Christmas,* an inspirational journey through ordinary days in December with the reader to find and impart extraordinary compassionate spirit to others in every day of the year.

This is the seventh book by author, M. J. Scott, USA. Her other volumes include *Journey to Fulfillment, Time on the Turn, Power Steering, Power Steering 2, Double Feature!* and the novel, *Sport's Alien Fantasy* co-authored with Daniel Wetta. Learn more about these on the author's webpage: <u>M. J. Scott webpage</u>

Made in the USA
Columbia, SC
30 September 2018